Thoughts of a Daydreamer

By Lisa McGhee Smith

Foreword by **Dorothy I. Height**,
author of ***Open Wide the Freedom Gates***
and Chair/President Emerita
National Council of Negro Women, Inc.

Copyright 2008 Lisa McGhee Smith
Washington, DC

*No part of this work may be copied or reproduced
in any fashion without the expressed written permission of
the author or her authorized representatives or agents*

Photo credit: Flower photographs by
Jon Sullivan, pdphoto.org

ISBN 978-1-4357-0417-6
Manufactured in the United States of America

Foreword

Gone is the idea of the daydreamer as one who, with eyes wide open, is engaged in daydreaming about a world that never existed when you read this collection of the "Thoughts of a Daydreamer". Lisa McGhee Smith in her daydreaming thoughts is sharply focused and visionary. Every poem is reality based. Her poems go beneath the surface to share the values and reactions in a wide range of life experiences. You will find yourself quickly identifying with her and wondering why you had not thought of something so similar to your own.

Lisa McGhee Smith moves from the universal to the intimate with ease. Whatever the issue or whoever the person, the time or the place, her spirituality comes through. You will enjoy reaching beyond denomination into the reality of faith.

Lisa McGhee Smith reminds us of the vital importance of valuing relationships and the depth of love of family as in her thoughts she embraces her own, one by one. This is refreshing at a time when so much and so many are taken for granted. You and I are the beneficiaries of words created by one who does not hesitate to express her faith in God and her commitment to people everywhere. Lisa McGhee Smith has enriched the library for all striving to live a life of meaning and purpose.

Dorothy I. Height

Chair/President Emerita
National Council of Negro Women, Inc.

Acknowledgements

There are numerous people I can thank for getting this project completed. To get one's inner thoughts from the mind to paper and then to the public takes the concerted efforts of many in front of and behind the scenes.

First to my Lord and Savior, Jesus Christ, I thank you for my life. I thank God for blessing me with His gift of love, salvation and expressing myself through words. I will be forever your true and faithful servant. Thank you Father.

I wish to thank my mama, Annie Lee McGhee, and late daddy, Charlie B. McGhee for giving me the loving experiences of which I can write about. They, through their quiet and loving spirit, instilled in me truth, integrity and love. I want to thank my sisters and brother, Yvonne Parham, Cassandra Simon, Dwight McGhee, Gwinnett Ladson and Cynthia Woodard for allowing me to be a spoiled baby sister and loving me anyway. They inspire me to write about loving relationships and support because they are the epitome of true family. Thank you Cynthia for sharing your family and home from which I composed some of my poetry.

I thank my dear friends from New Orleans who would listen to my poetry at work or while cooking gumbo and encourage me to continue with my writings. To my girl, Jeanine Lewis, who would listen to my thoughts before they were configured into the actual poems.

Thoughts of a Daydreamer

I sincerely thank Dr. Dorothy Irene Height for the encouraging support that she gave to me. Her advocacy and support for women of color will leave a legacy for all of us to build upon.

I especially thank my mother-in-law, Vivian L. Smith, who was not only responsible for this publication coming to fruition, but validated my work whenever her tears would flow while reading my poetry. Her vision of this project began before the thought entered my mind and I am so appreciative of her dedication and tireless effort in getting it completed. She is synonymous with love and I truly thank God for her everyday.

I thank my sons Julius III, Jamaal and Justin for being wonderful sons and my inspiration. Thank you for letting me be your mom in every sense of the word. Thanks for allowing me to love and nurture you, for being sources of my pride and being reasons God is on my speed dial.

Finally, yet importantly, I thank my husband Julius for loving me unconditionally. He has supported me from the very first poem I wrote and continues to encourage me to write even more. His love and support in all my endeavors in life are unparallel to any other and I truly thank him for always being right by my side in love and spirit.

Lisa McGhee Smith

Lisa McGhee Smith_____

Thoughts of a Daydreamer
—— *Contents* ——

Life
Disempowered	2
A Coach's Widow	4
Don't Be A Quitter	6
Choices	7
Betrayed	8
Emotions	10
Just Ask A Child	11
I'm Too Busy to Get Sick	12
Sad Eyes	13
Glimpses of Light	14
Fear and Friendship	15
Today I Will Cry	16
Keys of Life	18

Religious
Children's Prayers	20
Morning Prayer	21
Salvation	22
Knowing	24
Do You See What I See?	25
The Beautiful Body of Christ	26
Forgotten	27
What Does Christmas Really Mean?	28
6 Billion People	29
God Lent Us An Angel	30
Scared the Hell Out of Me	31
Still in Control	32
Happy Birthday Mt. Moriah	34
Attitude Adjustment	36
Looking for the Answers	38
God Ain't Through With Me Yet	40

Family
Mama	42
Tribute to Father	43
Baby Girl	44
Family	46

_____*Thoughts of a Daydreamer*

Thoughts of a Daydreamer
—— *Contents Continued*——

Family
Vivian's Love	47
A Mother's Love	48
Prayer Answered	49
Heeey Buddy	50
Jeanine	52
Here I Am	53
My Big Sister	54
Pride Overflowing	55
Ode to Cassandra	56
PMD MD Poem	58
To My Little Princess Brittney	60
To The Grandchildren of Vivian	62
Daughters in the Light	64
Always My Friend	66
God's Reflection	67

Love
Because I Said Yes	69
I Already Had You	70
My Precious Valentine	71
Missing You	72
Sweet Feeling	73
Grateful	74
How Much Do You Love Me?	76
Show Me How	77
What Is It About You?	78

General
Thoughts of a Daydreamer	81
Hello Brother	82
My Space	83
Tests	84
Pleasantville	85
Will You Step Away?	86
Pseudosuicide	87
Dreams	88
Journey Around the Sun	90

Lisa McGhee Smith_____

Life

Disempowered
A Coach's Widow
Don't Be A Quitter
Choices
Betrayed
Emotions
Just Ask A Child
I'm Too Busy to Get Sick
Sad Eyes
Glimpses of Light
Fear and Friendship
Today I Will Cry
Keys of Life

Thoughts of a Daydreamer

*Disempowered...
No More*

The alarm rings to start another day
Should I get up…or roll over and stay
I ponder the meaning of life
while staring at the ceiling trying to shake
that heavy, defeated, "what's the point" feeling

Why should I get up off my back
to use my skills making up for another's lack
Not to be acknowledged, appreciated or
adequately paid for the profits that my
knowledge and expertise made

Why should I give them another chance to
constantly remind me of my circumstance
Of being trapped, powerless and weak working
in a system
where my future seems bleak.

How do I fight back and regain some control
of a life that is threatening to take my soul?
How do I renew my lease on life and reclaim the
power that I surrendered to strife?

Will I continue to look down upon and speak
negatively about others' plans to progress?
Or listen intensely, take mental notes
and draw from their happiness

Lisa McGhee Smith

Will I continue to not support others' ventures
because of fear that I will be left even further
behind and still bound?
Or begin to invest in my own future
by believing what goes around will come around
Will I continue to treat humanity as if it owes
me the world because my education and training
don't match my paycheck?

Or not hold mankind responsible for my lot nor
buy into society's definition of whether
I'm successful or not

And will I continue to lay on my back
wallowing in self pity for the hand I've been
dealt but from this day forward, make a
vow to myself to view each day as
"training" to reclaim all the feelings of
disempowerment that I felt

I'm late for work

Thoughts of a Daydreamer

A Coach's Widow

October fifteen is the designated day
that basketball takes my husband away
Emotions mixed with joy and sadness
begins each year at Midnight Madness

Practices beginning at six a.m.
and again at three
Players getting in shape-that's how it has to be
Watching tapes and individual workouts
"When are you coming home?!" I begin to shout

Letter writing, recruiting visits and calls
I just don't get to see my husband at all
Toast in his mouth as he's walking out the door
Eating popcorn while watching games
sitting on the floor

Returning late from a road game
and feeling tired
I hope we won so no one gets fired
Everyone knows to stay out of his way
if poor shooting and bad calls led to poor play

I sit in my seat at each home game
Trying not to be a bother
as I listen to fans occasionally
question the decision of my children's father

Our livelihood depends on a few young men
being disciplined, playing well and getting ranked
number ten

Lisa McGhee Smith

Each game has a lot of stress and strife
But such is the life of a coach's wife

My soul is grieving so I wear all black
I'm not asking for much...just my husband back
You see this is an annual routine that is in tow
This is the time I become a coach's widow

Thoughts of a Daydreamer

Don't Be A Quitter

Life will bring you its share of highs and lows
There will be times when it seems
like anything goes
Unfair decisions will make you feel bitter
But don't give up—don't be a quitter

Times will get rough and
you'll ask what's the point
Disappointment may tempt you
to reach for that joint
But keep hanging tough and be a big hitter
Don't give up—don't be a quitter

Don't get discouraged if you missed the first try
Even the second and third misfire
may make you want to cry
Continue to fight even if your emotions lie in litter
But don't give up—don't be a quitter

When inconsistency and favoritism
makes you holler and scream
Don't let anyone take away your dream
Heed those words constructively from
the criticism critter
But don't give up—don't be a quitter

Life teaches many lessons as you journey through
Disaster, distress and disenchantment to name a few

So believe in your self let faith be a transmitter
And don't give up—don't be a quitter!

Lisa McGhee Smith

Choices

What was He thinking when
He chose my gender?
Why did she choose that name?
Breast milk or formula?
Should I wear ponytails or braids?
Will I choose eternal life?
Pads or tampons?
Who will I go with to the dance?
Should I smoke it or not?
Will I study hard or blow it off?
Cheerleading or band?
Should I go to Harvard or Yale?
Will I lose my virginity in this place?
Doctor or lawyer?
Will I accept the job abroad?
Who will meet my parents?
Should I say yes now?
Which car should we buy?
Three children or four?
What was He thinking when
He chose their gender?

Thoughts of a Daydreamer

Betrayed

There was a time when you were the
crown jewel of my existence
You housed my mind and my essence
and we stayed in top form through persistence

You demanded attention whenever you
made an appearance
Cat calls and long gazes were
always in abundance

But at some point you decided you
have had enough
Time and its spouse, Aging, made it tough

Hair that used to be long, thick and black
is now the residence of "silver sneakers"
who just began to unpack

Pearly white teeth when exposed would
light up a room
Now lie in state next to their replacements
in a half-filled glass "tomb"

Supple breasts whose firmness needed not the
support of a bra
have hitchhiked a ride on gravity
heading south
as if the floor is a Palm Springs resort and spa

Lisa McGhee Smith

A toned tummy made which <u>color</u> bikini
the decision of the day

Now appears to be the hiding place
of where a refugee decided to stay

A firm backside that off of it
a coin could bounce
has decided to become an electromagnetic
cellulite center where every
ounce of fat is attracted to pounce

And legs that were once shapely,
sexy and smooth
and could stop traffic
won't walk three blocks without cramping
not even for Denzel or Ben Affleck

That's why I feel betrayed by my body
who decided it didn't care
that my mind wasn't ready to
give Old Man Time its share

So, I will remain in combat
giving and receiving scar for scar
Body, you may have won this battle
but I will win the war!

Thoughts of a Daydreamer

Emotions

Emotions are like the wind
blowing east or west, north or south
and sometimes not at all

Emotions are like a roller coaster
sometimes up, sometimes down
competent to give exhilarating thrills
capable of producing nausea

Emotions are like weapons
cutting the heart to its core
shooting down the efforts of forgiveness

Emotions are the soul's language
speaking to the world
communicating the present state of mind

Lisa McGhee Smith

Just Ask A Child

In this world when one has to look hard
to find the truth
Because TV, magazines and retailers are
selling to your inner youth
A straight answer you cannot get even
if you searched a mile
But if you really want to know, just ask a child

The salesperson said I looked fabulous
in the hat
Until my child asked, "What made you go
and buy that?!"

The streaks in my hair were intended to distract
from my face's fine lines
Until my child said, "But I was supposed to go
as the Bride of Frankenstein!"

I finally felt comfortable to wear the red dress
with enough room to wiggle
Until my child said cartoons were not as funny as
watching the fat on my bottom jiggle

And when I look in the mirror questioning if yet
another wrinkle is on my face
My child sits studiously on the bed and asks, "Are you
and Grandma having a race?"

So, if you want to really know the truth about
yourself and you're tired of all the lies
Be prepared to see yourself through the eyes of an
innocent child!

Thoughts of a Daydreamer

I'm Too Busy to Get Sick And I Ain't Got Time To Die

Beep Beep Beep Beep...the alarm screams to me
"Get up...Get going...There are places you have to be"
But I just got in bed with unfinished work piled high
I want to sleep 5 more minutes right where I lie

My body wants to slow down.
It's tired and needs a rest
But I don't have time to stop right now
My to do list is from east to west

"Busy running here and stopping there
has worn me out," I sigh
But I'm just so busy that I can't get sick
And I ain't got time to die

I've got errands to run, meals to make
And homework to check tonight
Calls to return, games to watch
And laundry that's reached a new height

"You'd better slow down. You're gonna get ill."
I hear them constantly cry
But I'm too busy to get sick
And I ain't got time to die

We are never given more than we can bear
and my unfinished tasks make me want to cry
But God gives me strength and keeps me going 'cause
I'm too busy to get sick
And I ain't got time to die

Lisa McGhee Smith

Sad Eyes

I look at those eyes
as dark as the bluest shade of black
perfectly round and flawless in detail

I look at those eyes
with an endless well of tears
that keep them glistening in the sunlight

I look at those eyes
that have seen more disappointment and pain
than a village of people

I look at those eyes
that now see life
with a dullness

I look at those eyes
those sad eyes
and wish the spark of innocence would return

Oh what sad eyes

Thoughts of a Daydreamer

Glimpses of Light

Is that a smile I feel crawling up my face
As if my lifting burdens are pulling the
corners of my mouth upward

The fruit being an expression of promise
which gives me strength to cope
with the struggles of life that are
weighing me down

Is that a glimpse of light
peeping around the bend
violating the total darkness of oppression,
despair and hopelessness

Is that a glimpse of light
peering into the window bringing radiance
to a heavy laden soul
offering it rest

The reality of the situation now interludes in the
shade created by
the glimpses of light
peeking over the horizon

Lisa McGhee Smith

Fear and Friendship

An elderly lady asked me once "Do you mind if I cry?
I'm lying here in this bed and I don't know the reason why."

I proceeded to explain the reason for her location
How she had forgotten she couldn't walk alone
And fell trying to get to her "vocation"

"I don't know why I'm here. I don't know why I'm in pain.
What if my daughter can't find me? I feel like I'm going insane."

I did my best to comfort her, to eliminate all her fears
As I held her hand and caressed her arm trying to hold back my tears

She looked at me again and asked, "Do you mind if I cry?
I don't think I belong here. I don't want this to be the place that I die."

I reassured her again that she was not here to expire
But to heal, regain her strength and relight that inner fire

She smiled at me as I saw some of her tension begin to end
Then she reached for my hand saying
"Thank you for being so kind to me.
Thank you for being my friend."

Thoughts of a Daydreamer

Today I Will Cry

Today I will cry
and not hold back my tears
when I wake up to an empty abode
wishing my loneliness disappears

Today I will cry
and not hold back my tears
when I think of the recent stress
I've endured because of peers

Today I will cry
and not hold back my tears
when the criticism from a loved one
Has cut using unforgiving shears

Today I will cry
and not hold back my tears
when the one I've planned my future with
Has decided to switch gears

Today I will cry
and not hold back my tears
when my little failures
Bring out audible cheers

Today I will cry
and not hold back my tears
when my finances are in crisis
and the due date nears

Lisa McGhee Smith

Today I will cry
and not hold back my tears
when I see the other lover
and the green eyed monster rears

Today I will cry
and not hold back my tears
when a confession of untruth
just validates my fears

Today I will cry
and not hold back my tears
when I finally realize my priceless self worth
and its accompanying joy in the coming years

Thoughts of a Daydreamer

Keys of Life

Behind every door
exists mysteries and opportunities to explore

Life gifts us with keys to open every locked door
to find out what this universe has in store

We oft are not equipped after the latch unclicks
to face a world which at every turn is a wall of bricks

But thank God He sent an angel
who chimes with every breath
whose presence has an overture
drenched in wisdom and wealth

Her loving and caring spirit has given us
encouragement
to shield fiery darts of strife
The examples she has set after
all these years are our

KEYS OF LIFE

Lisa McGhee Smith

Religious

Children's Prayers
Morning Prayer
Salvation
Knowing
Do You See What I See?
The Beautiful Body of Christ
Forgotten
What Does Christmas Really Mean?
6 Billion People
God Lent Us An Angel
Scared the Hell Out of Me
Still in Control
Happy Birthday Mt. Moriah
Attitude Adjustment
Looking for the Answers
God Ain't Through With Me Yet

Thoughts of a Daydreamer

Children's Prayers

Thank you God for your son Jesus
He is my friend and I love Him so
I want to make Him very happy
So off to church I go

I will be your friend
I'll play with you today
Jesus is your friend too
He's with you all the way

I don't like carrots
I don't like peas
But I have food in front of me
That God gave to make me strong
So I can last all day long

Thank you God for mommy and daddy
They take good care of me
Thank you God for sister and brother
They also will agree

I feel very sad today
I really want to cry
And when things don't go my way
I feel better when again I try

Lisa McGhee Smith

Morning Prayer

As I open my eyes to wake
'Tis the Lord my soul's to thank
Today, my purpose is to fulfill
The loving work of God's will.

Thoughts of a Daydreamer

Salvation

I didn't think it would be like this
I never knew this feeling I own
I couldn't begin to tell the world the
vast joy and happiness in this zone

I thought I would have to give it all up
that I would have no more fun
But then I decided to place my trust
in God 's only begotten Son

The Love was felt immediately
The Peace sensed deep within
The revelation unveiled which uncovered
my life that was about to begin

The scriptures now had new meaning
Those promises were made to me
The instructions of love and righteousness
were illuminated for me to see

The tests and trials I go through
are ones I'm willing to accept
Because I know they are preparing me
for the promises that will be kept

There are times when I battle
my flesh and spirit are at war
But my comfort rest knowing the
Lord will be victorious by far

Lisa McGhee Smith

You may not see me in the street
handing out a tract or two
But I must share with all the world
what salvation can do for you

Thoughts of a Daydreamer

Knowing

How do you know that you know that you
know you are blessed?

When God allows you to feel an unbelievable joy
within the midst of a time of stress

How do you know that you know that
you know God loves you?

When He makes sure you are surrounded by
people whose unconditional love shines through

How do you know that you know that you know
you are favored?

When during the good and bad, highs and lows
Your faith does not waiver

How do you know that you know that you know
you are destined?

When during the fatiguing pursuit of your dreams
His arms are always there to rest in

Lisa McGhee Smith

Do You See What I See?

NATURE lets me see
green, brown, red, purple and gold

THE SKY lets me see
blue, gray, yellow and orange

MY BRAIN lets me see my favorites
turquoise, magenta and violet

SOCIETY lets me see only
black and white

GOD lets me see
no color

Thoughts of a Daydreamer

The Beautiful Body of Christ

We are the beautiful body of Christ

We are His hands
when reaching out to others

We are His feet
when walking in truth

We are His eyes
when seeing the needs of people

We are His mouth
when speaking the gospel of Christ

We are His ears
when hearing the prayer requests of saints

We are His back
when giving support to those in need

We are His heart
when loving unconditionally as He does

We have His mind
to be righteous
to be truthful
to intercede
to love
to be faithful

We are the beautiful body of Christ

Lisa McGhee Smith

Forgotten

Sometimes I feel like God has forgotten me
I've got so many troubles and trials
that an end I cannot see

I've prayed and prayed for God to deliver me
I've studied and obeyed-of which
I thought was the key
But sometimes I feel like God has forgotten me

I feel alone at times struggling all by myself
Times seem so bad that I can feel
a change in my health
I often wonder and cry out how can this be
Sometimes I feel like God has forgotten me

The Devil uses my emotions as
ammunition in his fight
to get me not to believe in God's powerful might

But I will be patient and wait on the Lord
I will use His word like a two edged sword
to cut down the Devil as he tries
to plant seeds of unbelief
I will use all my weapons until God sends me relief

I find comfort in knowing that God knows my case
And I gain strength daily every time I seek His face

Whenever I attend my own pity party
thinking I am forgotten
I just remember to meditate on His word
Then the Devil's words become null and
void as they come out rotten

Thoughts of a Daydreamer

What Does Christmas Really Mean?

When you think about this day do you sigh?
Were you shopping for gifts in July?

Does this time of year bring out your worst?
If you saw one more Santa would you burst?

Does this season put your credit cards in ICU
for undeserved toys or
just to get something new?

We have traveled far from the reason
why we should really celebrate this season

There is One who has already given us a
gift money cannot buy
A present more valuable than
precious gems piled high
Unwrap this Gift-remove the paper,
ribbons and bows
to find magnificent peace and joy for your soul

The true meaning of Christmas is not stressful
and full of financial fuss
but a time to give back to others
through love, forgiveness
and sharing the gift God gave to us

Merry Christmas and Happy Holidays

Lisa McGhee Smith

6 Billion People

There are six billion people in the world
And not one looks like me
Now that is just simply amazing
How do you think that could be?

Someone might have the same color eyes and
shaped nose as me
Another might have the same cheekbones
If I looked very hard I just might find
another with my exact skin tone

Knowing that I was uniquely made
no match with anyone on earth
truly makes me proclaim to all
how deserving the Creator is of His worth!

Thoughts of a Daydreamer

God Lent Us An Angel

God lent us an angel
while we still occupy this earth

God sent us an angel
giving another demonstration of His worth

God gave us an angel
to show an example of His way

God gave us an angel
because He knew about today

God lent us an angel
who was made perfect in His eyes

God sent us an angel
even though now we must say goodbye

God sent us an angel
who was made of love, compassion and praise

God sent us an angel
who always had holy hands to raise

God sent us an angel
who He equipped with a majestic voice

God lent us an angel
that has gone home to rejoice

God lent us this angel
for a season to brighten our lives
And now He has called her back over yon'
so she can hear Him say, "Valerie, well done."

In memory of Valerie Battles at her homegoing
December 23, 2006

Lisa McGhee Smith

Scared The Hell Out of Me

I woke up this morning with no feeling in my leg
It scared the hell out of me
I sat down at breakfast and nearly choked
on an egg
It scared the hell out of me

The news said someone was killed
three houses down
It scared the hell out of me
Drugs have destroyed the neighborhood
in my hometown
It scared the hell out of me

I read HIV/AIDS is the leading cause of death in
young Black women
It scared the hell out of me
I walked up one flight of stairs
and lost my breath
It scared the hell out of me

The preacher said I'd better live right
before it's too late
It scared the hell out of me
He said repent, accept Christ
and get rid of that hate
It scared the hell out of me

Now I'm saved, sanctified and Heaven bound you
see
Because I got the HELL scared out of me

Thoughts of a Daydreamer

Still in Control

I asked the Lord, "Why are You sending me
through all these troubling times?"
Before one is over another comes around

I know I haven't been an angel or
a saint all my life
But I felt I don't deserve all this strife

I said, "Lord, do what You have to
do to purify me
But does my family have to suffer, can't you let
them be?"

And the Lord revealed to my heart
that these tests and trials were just the start

Of a journey that would take me to a place
that I've never been before

A place where He would pour His love out
if I'd just open up the door

He said, "I want to bring out the best in you
But I promise I will see you through."

"I want to bring out the Job in you"

You see, Satan has to ask permission to test you
And I have to say that it's okay
But I'll build a hedge around
you…you know I care
because I will never give you
more than you can bear

Lisa McGhee Smith

So, know that I'm in control
even though you're going through hard times

Know that I'm still in control
and I promise you'll make it through

Just remember that I'm in control
of your destiny

So settle down, keep your faith
And know I'll see you through
Yes, know I'll see you through
Just believe that I will see you through

Thoughts of a Daydreamer

Happy Birthday Mt. Moriah

We gather at this appointed season
to celebrate God's love which is the reason
one hundred and twenty years ago He spoke to
twenty six women and men
to branch off and go where He would send

The first house of worship where
they would meet
was in Southwest DC on Second Street
As the church grew under the leadership of
Reverends Scott and Dent,
it was all in the news...
Mt. Moriah needed more pews!

In 1925, through Reverend Randolph's vision, a
fourth sanctuary was designed
And as the church kept growing, they
moved Northeast
to the present temple on
East Capitol Street's line

After Reverend Williams' project
Together We Build
came Reverend Hailes
whose Venture in Faith project
was a beacon of light
Then the Lord sent Reverend Dalton,
His precious
saint from Madison Heights

Lisa McGhee Smith

Those twenty six who sat on that
branch many years
ago were united in Christ, its true
They listened to Jesus who said "I will
remain united to you."

Always showing God's standard of living
in our walk
with the purpose of leading others to Christ in
our talk
while we spread the gospel of our Lord
is the church's mission we work toward

Mt. Moriah continues to remain
in the True Vine
and in her, the world's light shines
allowing the Gardener to snip and prune
to bear fruit and hear God's pleasure soon!

Thoughts of a Daydreamer

Attitude Adjustment

I woke up this morning mad at the world
Upset that I had to get up and uncurl

I grumbled walking to the bathroom
Mad that the light was so bright
Glancing at the mirror
Noticing a frightful sight

After showering, I tossed clothes everywhere
Frustrated that I couldn't find a thing to wear

I began thinking about my work place
And all the people who got on my nerves
Mentally giving each a piece of my mind
That each one deserves

I discarded my half-eaten breakfast
from lack of appetite
Exasperated that I didn't count the carbs right

When I glanced at the clock realizing again
I would be running late
I rushed to my car consumed
with frustration and hate

I sat in my car surrounded
by a deafening silence
And the next sounds I heard
were through His guidance

"My child, you need an attitude of gratitude" was
what my spirit heard
"I have explained it all in my precious Word."

Lisa McGhee Smith

I sat and thought about all my blessings
That escape my heart when mind and soul are wrestling

As I reflected on the morn,
I saw every blessing being reborn:
I slept peacefully in a bed and not on the ground
Comfort, warmth and shelter all around
God woke me up instead of an eternal sleep
A right mind, sight and strength He let me keep
Hot water to bathe and clothes from many a choice
A job to make provision and a place to have a voice
He gave me food to eat that I didn't have to beg for
And a car to drive so I wouldn't have to walk no more

That was just a morning's worth of blessings
Just the iceberg's tip
A grain of sand's worth according to the vastness of His Lordship

So from this day forward I changed my attitude to one of gratitude
Lord, You are my King and I want to sing
How great Your worth in all the earth
And I will give You praise all of my days

Thoughts of a Daydreamer

Looking for the Answers

It appears that all is right in my world
Life filled with diamonds and pearls
It appears that there are no struggles in my life
An existence absent of any stress or strife

But everything that glitters ain't gold
and all ain't what it seems
In private my daily battles are sometimes taken to extremes
My flesh and spirit are constantly at war
which leaves me in situations that are bizarre

I've tried to pursue happiness
from riches and fame
Days filled with unfulfillment,
nights filled with shame
It wasn't until a revelation
was softly spoken to me
that this pursuit I was chasing
would never be reached
What an epiphany!

The glory I wanted only belongs to One
who was loving enough to give His only Son
And even now that I know His will
I battle daily with the Enemy who's trying to kill

So don't look to me for the answers when it seems
you can't cope
But go directly to the One
who will fill you with hope

Lisa McGhee Smith

If He sends you back my way
I will share a testimony of my tests day to day
Of how each fire appeared to be the one
that would burn
And after I made it
through…the lessons I learned

If you're looking for the answers stop
gazing ahead and look up
Ask Him personally what you should do
and I promise He'll get back to you

Thoughts of a Daydreamer

God Ain't Through With Me Yet

I know when you look at me
your head shakes in unbelief
You can't believe I'm still hanging in there
with no signs of relief

You can't believe with all the
dejection, disappointment and despair I've felt
That I haven't quit and given up
because of the hand I was dealt

You look at my life and wonder
"What's the point?"
when you see how sickness, poverty and failure all
lie in joint

You ask when will I realize my life has no hope
as I journey up the world's slippery slope

But when you come closer I'll tell you not to fret
'Cause God ain't through with me yet

This temporary suffering I can endure
As it makes my faith grow more mature

My hope isn't in worldly gain
But what Jesus did when He left his blood stain

You see I don't mind going through
test after test
'Cause when God gets through
I know I'll be blessed

Lisa McGhee Smith

Family

Mama
Tribute to Father
Baby Girl
Family
Vivian's Love
A Mother's Love
Prayer Answered
Heeey Buddy
Jeanine
Here I Am
My Big Sister
Pride Overflowing
Ode to Cassandra
PMD MD Poem
Always My Friend
To My Little Princess Brittney
To The Grandchildren of Vivian
Daughters in the Light
Always My Friend
God's Reflection

Thoughts of a Daydreamer

Mama

You were blessed with a special ability
to love your children

From the moment of conception we were loved
and we know we will be loved
until the end of time
We have felt your love...
in the words of encouragement and praise
you give each of us
in the self-sacrificing decisions
you made to provide for us
in the support of your presence
whenever we needed you around
in the flavorfulness of the home cooked meals
you made for us
in the examples you set as a Christian, mother
and friend for us
in the unconditional way we now
love our children and family that you taught us

It is amazing how you can make each of
us feel like we have all your love as if we
all were an only child

We were given an invaluable gift from God
to have been blessed with such a mother as you

Thank you for being such a wonderful, loving
and caring woman

Thank you for being our mother

Lisa McGhee Smith

Tribute to Father

It is yet another Father's Day
We're filled with many words to say
Material possessions are not enough
To express appreciation for all the stuff
You do for each and everyone of us

We looked in Brooks, Lords and Saks
For the coolest fanciest gift packs
But could not get off to a good start
Because they were not selling our hearts

Julius, the Lord set you apart from all the rest
Because He knew we could love you best
Today, we are not bearing gifts from the stores above
'Cause God has already given us the ultimate gifts of love
Yes, He gave Jesus Christ to the world too
But to our family He gave us…
YOU!

HAPPY FATHER'S DAY

Thoughts of a Daydreamer

Baby Girl

If I had to choose my most favorite
memory of you
It would be difficult because they all are
precious and now seem too few

I can remember sitting on your lap holding
your hand when I was four
Feeling happy, safe and secure in your arms
feeling your strength down to my core

I can remember as a little girl acting
like your secretary
Writing down the minutes from
everyone's quotes
Scribbling on your pad taking illegible notes

I can remember the first time I ate a burger
from Shug Gal's café
"Add some fried taters and dress it with
mustard", I heard you say
I felt special eating something different that
didn't come from my grandfather's garden
Sitting at a table not my mama's drinking milk
not out of a carton

I often try to forget the only time you
had to discipline me
My actions caused you to question a store
owner's memory and integrity
I could not appreciate how you stood up for me

Lisa McGhee Smith

through the words of your mouth
And how you took a chance on not becoming
strange fruit in the South

I remember waiting on Friday evenings
for you to come home from work
Then jumping in your lap to read the latest
book was my biggest perk

Your presence during my teenage years was really
a blur
I didn't have much time for you as many new emotions began to stir

I can remember seeing you once in attendance at
my basketball games
Pleased and proud to have you in the stands
made getting that triple double a breeze
as everyone clapped their hands

And I remember the only time you've ever
danced was with me on my wedding day
Your baby girl will cherish that moment and
In her heart it will stay.

Thoughts of a Daydreamer

Family

When you are born
the world might not be aware
of your arrival on this earth
but your family is right there

And growing up when times get tough
it might seem more than you can bear
Friends will come and go
but your family is right there

Working hard and accomplishing the impossible
will go unnoticed by those who do not care
But pats on the back and words of praise
will come from your family who's there

Stating new ventures or in a temporary bind
won't phase those with much to spare
But even when times get tough
your family is right there

There is something special about that genetic bond
that is so unique and rare
There is no other connection quite like family
who will always be right there

Lisa McGhee Smith

Vivian's Love

It's the time of the year
to spread love and good cheer
The world will be laughing and full of joy
Each child waiting for that special toy

It is time to let our loved ones know
how much we care with a big fancy bow
We might get a car, a ring or just a dove
but nothing is more cherished
than Vivian's Love

She mixes wisdom with patience
in the absence of tense
and makes being a mother
seem so common sense

Yes, we would like a tie or a game or a new stove
but nothing would be more cherished than Vivian's
Love

We are so lucky to be blessed with you
'cause we get Christmas all the year through
Yes, we honor and worship God's
love from above
but after, there is nothing more cherished than
Vivian's Love

Thoughts of a Daydreamer

A Mother's Love

A mother's love is always obvious in the way she looks at you or holds you in her arms or smiles when she's caressing your face

A mother's love is also there when she cooks your favorite food or says the perfect words to comfort you or make all your hurts-physical and emotional-feel better

A mother's love is not as overt to her children when she says no to staying past curfew or buying the expensive toy or in the many sacrifices she makes

A mother's love is often seen in the decisions she makes to be the best mother she can be

To be the best mother means first, being the best person you can be to your children every day

There comes a time in a mother's life that she must choose to be the best person by choosing to keep the essence of who she is intact

-by choosing her sanity over the status quo
-by choosing to walk away from the unchanged, tradition and misery

The greatest expression of a mother's love is to choose a life full of peace, love and happiness so it will be manifested in her children's lives

HAPPY MOTHER'S DAY

Lisa McGhee Smith

Prayer Answered

Lord, I stand before You now
Humbled by your loving Grace
Thanking you for your gift of love
which is standing before my face

Lord, you have always known my heart
To love and be loved by someone set apart
It was my heart's desire to do Your will
when You told my spirit to wait and be still

I'd ask You, "Lord, when are you going to
send my soul mate?"
But Your Holy Spirit kept sending
the message to wait

A woman of God would be my wish
someone to honor, love and cherish
someone to pray with, laugh with...
Who would not be a bore
someone who I could smile at and
absolutely adore

Well, the Lord said, "Kevin, your wait is over.
All the qualities you've asked
for...I've got it covered.
I'm giving you a love which is kind,
not envious and suffereth long
bearing, believing, hoping
and enduring all things is her song...

I've sent you My child and My servant who has my favor to
live joyfully with...creating
memories to savor

Kevin, I've answered your prayers to not live your life
barren

So, I sent...your beautiful wife...KAREN!"

Thoughts of a Daydreamer

Heeey Buddy

Heeey Buddy,
As I reflect on your life in the past
Many thoughts and memories run
through so fast
You've departed from this world and left us here to
stay so through these words, I want to express to
you what I have to say

Whenever we talked you were full of advice
Leaving me with wisdom more than to suffice

You would show me grace, mercy and love
Making me feel special as does the
One from Above
And when Kevin and I went to places we should not
have been
I remember the love (preceded by the lectures and
of course...the discipline)

Heeey Buddy,
Your generosity was so great that when you had a
nickel, you'd give away three cents
You'd give us anything if we asked and I never felt
uncomfortable or tense

You were a loving man, full of vigor
who enjoyed life
You taught me to always take care of my family
and to always love my wife

Lisa McGhee Smith

You made all of us feel like part of your family
Your heart was so full of love,
obvious to anyone who could see

Heeey Buddy,
Biologically you were blessed with two children,
a grandson and a great grandchild
But there are countless other "children" you've
touched...the line could extend a mile

You treated us with love just like
we were your own
I appreciate Regina and Kevin letting their
father be out on "loan"

Unc,
I don't know when it will be my time to stand at
the Pearly Gates with knees like putty
But I know you'll be there smiling
with open arms saying..."Heeey Buddy!"

Thoughts of a Daydreamer

JEANINE

Jesus with His gentle hand comforted me in this
    new land
Expressing His love through a friend He
    personally chose from heaven to send "She'll
Always be there for you and
Never let you down whose
Incredible family values are always strong and
    sound
Numberless are the reasons I chose her to be your
    friend
Extraordinary sisterly love she'll give again and
    again"

Lisa McGhee Smith

Here I Am

I've been anxiously waiting to meet
my new family.
My mama, my daddy and my brother
Christopher sounded like neat people
I couldn't wait to see

The Lord told me I'd still be under His care
as He sent me to answer my brother's prayer
I knew I was coming to say hi
Before I was a gleam in my daddy's eye

I know I gave my mama fits
in her womb as I tossed and kicked
I heard her say more than once,
"I need my legs stretched...quick!"

Well, January 18th was my original date
But I decided that was just too late.
So at 5 pounds, 11 ounces and 18 inches long
The Lord said, "Go ahead, meet your family...
You'll be strong"

I said "Okay Lord, You're in charge" as
I prepared to meet my "fam"
I'm finally coming...I'm finally coming
And BAM...

Here I Am!

Thoughts of a Daydreamer

My Big Sister

My earliest memories of you
Date back to when I was one, maybe two
I stood circled by my sisters and brother
Rooting for me to pick one over the other

You played with me and cared for me
Doing it out of love—never charging a fee
After making mud pies, playing house was the feature
And when we played school, you were always the teacher!

You were my role model and you didn't even know it
I mimicked all your traits down to your quick wit
As you grew older and more independent not to mention
I still never had to starve for your attention

As I grew older, peer pressure followed on cue
I'd reflect on my big sister and ask
What would Toolee do?

Our lives have kept us in separate
parts of the South
But never too far to hear your big mouth
Our sisterly bond is stronger than any other
Woven by bands of love for our parents,
God and each other.

I Love You Big Sister!

Lisa McGhee Smith

Pride Overflowing

I've loved you
Since the first time I met you
Not for you but for whom you were a part of...

I watched you toddle, then walk, then sprint...
Watching you explore and experience
new feelings

You challenged me to love you unconditionally
Despite the array of circumstances you faced

Through your emotions
I have felt your pain, fear and disappointment
As well as your happiness, joy and pride

It has been an immeasurable delight to watch
You grow emotionally, physically and spiritually

As I look back over the years and see myself
Standing quietly in the background...
I cannot recall the moment I began
to love you for you

Julius, your accomplishments thus far
have created
An overflow of pride, love and joy in my heart

And...
I thank you for allowing me to be
a part of your life
Facilitating your metamorphosis to manhood

CONGRATULATIONS!

Thoughts of a Daydreamer

Ode to Cassandra

Back in 1954, gas was a nickel maybe more

Poodle skirts and bobby socks were on the
fashion scene
Smoky and the Miracles had the heart
of every teen

General "Ike" ran the country with an iron fist
And little "Miss Brown" took on the
Board of Education
as Thurgood Marshall dished out the assist

But little did the world know that a baby with two
months yet to grow
decided she was ready to fly like a bird
made her debut on May the third

Yes, she came a few weeks too soon
Was it too dark in there?
Maybe it was a full moon
Her little arms and legs revealed
her small bones
But one thing for sure…
that head was fully grown

Well, she finally grew into that body
to match her crown
This was the first sign that nothing
would keep her down

Lisa McGhee Smith

She soaked up knowledge everywhere
she turned
Any and everything was what she
wanted to learn

She believed in fairness, equality for all or none
Her protests heard on Highway 166 from
Bowdon to the Board of Education

Blessed with beauty and brains
shining in the light
Studying molecular biology by day and
Miss Albany State by night

And although her journey of life hasn't
turned out like she dreamed
Over time, with love and support, she realized life
is not as bad as it seems

That ambitious, strong willed personality will keep
her doing all she can
but if you want to hear God laugh,
just tell Him your plans

Cassandra is an excellent role model
and the epitome of perseverance
She is loved...she is respected...
by those who hold her dearest

We Love You Cassandra,
Happy 50th Birthday!

Thoughts of a Daydreamer

PMD MD Poem

It all began six years ago
Employees of the Foundation ready to blow
We needed an outlet to let off steam
Tired of hearing "work as a team"

So we got together and made a decision
To create the Physical Medicine Department-
Minority Division
Fine African-Americans and one Latino
Began partying at Christmas on the down low

We partied at Donna and Ben's after Gwen's
Food and spirits were a go, just ask Pablo
Laughing and joking the whole night long
Fuzzy duck-ducky fuzz
had many cursing that song

We cleaned up our act and moved Uptown
Eating hors-d'oeuvres, listening to jazz in
our semi-formal gowns
Chef barbecuing shrimp, frying crab
cakes and carving ham

The PMD-MD's "Twelve Days of
Christmas" because the hottest jam

Lisa McGhee Smith

A great time was had that night in December
So we did it again for Another Affair
to Remember
We honored our friend Reatha,
many praises did she get
And we finished it off with fried
bananas in a skillet

This gala has become an annual event
We look forward to time with friends well spent
It doesn't take a rocket scientist to see
How much fun this is going to be

So tonight, you do the math and see the addition
Of one more spectacular party by
The Physical Medicine Department-
Minority Division

Thoughts of a Daydreamer

To My Little Princess Brittney: Blossoming Princess

From the moment you entered this world
Watching your life blossom has been a joy
-Delightful, Amusing, Exciting

Your uniqueness was evident as a toddler
when you clearly communicated your desires
even before the words were formed

You were a blossoming flower

Each year as time went by
I saw your character develop

As your parents sowed seeds of love,
I saw you grow...
a petal of caring for your siblings
a petal of kindness for your community
a petal of humility in your life
a petal of love for our God

I watched you flourish into the exquisite
flower you are today

Lisa McGhee Smith

And as you make your debut to society
They will see a young lady
whose beauty illuminates the room
and grace represents royalty...
My little princess

Your tiara embeds the jewels of
intelligence, creativity, love, graciousness and
exceptionality

I am privileged to unveil your wonderful
qualities to everyone and
my heart is outpouring with pride

Thoughts of a Daydreamer

To The Grandchildren of Vivian L. Smith
What if?

I was **pondering** the mysteries of life one day
wondering what if your lives had
gone another way

Without **blinking** while staring
straight at the wall
I was **thinking** about how good life
has been to y'all

Imagining what would be different...
what wouldn't be true
The **badgering** of my thoughts left me with many
a clue

What would your life be like...
uneventful or full of strife?
What if your Grandma Vivian
had not been in your life

...**daring** to expose you to many
of life's treasures
caring enough to offer them for your pleasure

...being patient while you looked for your
independence around the next curve
Even though you're very close to
getting on her last nerve

Lisa McGhee Smith

...being **wealthy** enough to afford
you unexpected gifts
and **healthy** enough to travel, play and do many
leg lifts

...always **dice-less** when gambling with your
financial situations
because **price-less** is the value she places on your
future and education

...feeling your pain down to her core
being able to sense it as soon as you walk
through her door

...**knowing** the minute all of you were born, days
she always remembers
showing love and concern every time,
from January to December

...role modeling through her church,
social and civic duties
being a good example to you and all youth

...being **grateful** to you God for you and her other
blessings
being **faithful** to God through
trials and tough lessons

Who knows what book your life would have read
if God had given your Grandma
to another family instead

One thing I know to be true...
is that your Grandma Vivian is a big part of you!

Thoughts of a Daydreamer

Daughters in the Light

You stand before us radiant, as our light
Your loving character makes the
whole room bright
We watch you fight battles with
courage and might
We smile as you climb and soar to new heights

How blessed we are to have another mother
Whose values we love and share
One that thinks family always comes first
One who loves and cares

The love that we felt emanating from you
Made us feel honored, cherished
and special all anew
Expressing to many your love, from your
heart through each lip
And never using "in-law"
to describe our relationship

We are recognized, while in your company,
as extensions of you
Your halo beaming love, wisdom
and compassion, too
We stand reflecting your standards as cultured as a
string of pearls
Inwardly beaming with pride as we hear
whispers saying,
"those are Vivian's girls"

Lisa McGhee Smith

It is often said that men choose their soul mates
who are most like their mothers
They choose that special someone
who is unlike all the others

If that is true...
How proud we stand as daughters in the light
—a reflection of a strong righteous woman
like you!

Thoughts of a Daydreamer

Always My Friend

Long before you ever met me,
I was your friend

Long before I ever hugged you,
I was your friend

Long before we first played together,
I was your friend

Therefore, I will always cherish the day
you decided to become my friend, also

My friend Jamaal,
whom I watched stand quietly as you observed
with wide eyes life around you

My friend Jamaal,
whom I respected as you maintained your
individuality among the majority

My friend Jamaal,
whose artistic gift from God
always leaves me in awe

My friend Jamaal,
who has waited your due and
reached this major milestone in your life

Jamaal…Always my pride
Always my son
Always my friend

Lisa McGhee Smith

God's Reflection

When trying to express how much you
mean to us we have a difficult time knowing
where to even begin
You see, much of what we are, how we are
and who we are is reflective of your role in our lives as our
advisor, mentor and friend

We are caring...
because we saw you show grace and mercy to those
less fortunate
We are loving...
because we saw you love your family
unconditionally
We are giving...
because we saw you give meat to the hungry, drink to the
thirsty, hospitality to
the stranger and clothes to the naked
We are wise...
because we saw you make good judgments with a
discerning heart
We are compassionate...
because we saw you always expressing a deep feeling of love
and concern for
others' needs and difficulties
We are courageous...
because we saw you face many trials and dangers
with God's strength
We are truthful...
because we heard you speak with righteousness
what was true and accurate

But mostly we are thankful...
because God has shown us favor and kindness when
he made you our mother

We are a reflection of God
because God is reflected in you

Thoughts of a Daydreamer

Love

Because I Said Yes
I Already Had You
My Precious Valentine
Missing You
Sweet Feeling
Grateful
How Much Do You Love Me?
Show Me How
What Is It About You?

Lisa McGhee Smith

Because I Said Yes

Sleeping late
Feeling great
No signs of stress
...Because I said yes

Walking by me so fine
Adoration in my eyes
Making me feel my best
...Because I said yes

Vacations in exotic places
Making love in tight places
Endless ecstasy I must confess
...Because I said yes

Nights of unadulterated bliss
Mornings beginning with a soft kiss
Days filled with memories of his thoughtfulness
...Because I said yes

Occasional glimpses into the future
Visions of gray hair, grandchildren and cruises
I am in this state of happiness
Because to his proposal...
I said yes!

Thoughts of a Daydreamer

I Already Had You

I've dreamed of you since the beginning of time
Having someone of my own who was mine...all mine
Someone who would always have my back
Someone who would pick me up and take up the slack

I dreamed of someone who could look into my eyes
And pull out any secrets I tried to hide
Someone who put my happiness first as his goal
Whose simple gestures are felt deep in my soul

I dreamed of someone who would grow wiser with me
Someone not afraid to tell me no 'cause that's how it has to be
Someone who could overlook my faults and help strengthen my weaknesses
Calm my fears and relieve my stresses

I dreamed of someone who would lighten my burden and help carry my load
Not someone who was stuck in selfish mode
Someone who would love me unconditionally down to my core
Someone I could watch sleeping and absolutely adore

I dreamed that dream once wishing it to come true
And when I woke up I realized…
I already had you

Lisa McGhee Smith

My Precious Valentine

Good morning, my love...How's my boo?
Even at dawn's rising, my first thought is of you
I want to announce on this designated
day of hearts
That your love always gets me off to a good start

You are my stars, my moon, and my sun
You fill my life with days and nights of fun
There are times I don't know what to do
Because of my overflowing love for you

I thank God for giving you to me
Your love, passion and thoughtfulness are
visible for the world to see
This lifetime is not enough to give all my best
So I shall continue to love you in the next

Baby, you rock my world and make me complete
There is no other attraction that can compete
Your heart and love I know are all mine
I love you so much my precious valentine!

Thoughts of a Daydreamer

Missing You

You left two days after my birthday
As I watched you walked away
A piece of my soul followed
And I was forever changed

I leave your clothes lying around
Craving your scent left behind
I sleep in your pajamas
Just to be near your skin

I lie in this king-sized bed
Without you it feels like a continent
I long to wrap my legs around yours
And cuddle within your curves

When I hear your voice daily
Whispering good morning and good night
My soul awakens, my heart sings and
My body responds with a tingle

Baby, my world is not the same without you
The day when we're back together
Cannot come soon enough
You ask: What's gotten into me?
...I'm just missing you

Lisa McGhee Smith

Sweet Feeling

When I hear his name
I hesitate
Is he near by? Do you see him?

When I see his face
my face lights up
There's something about his smile
that makes me smile too

When I hear his voice
my heart flutters
The way he says my name
is like poetry

When I feel his touch
my skin tingles
The strength I feel in his arms
makes me feel secure

When he looks at me
my beauty from within shines through
I feel like a museum painting
with its details bringing admiration and awe

And when I call his name
what joy I feel when he comes running
to tell me he feels the same way too

Thoughts of a Daydreamer

Grateful

When I say my daily prayers to the Lord
Being ungrateful for His many blessings,
I cannot afford
Along with our health and wealth
for which I give
Him thanks,
is my eternal gratitude for you that
gets the highest rank

Julius, I thank you for............
The first compliment you gave me
which made me smile
The friendship and advice
(all I had to do was dial)
The peace and protection I feel
when you are near
The tender moments that are still so dear
The fun days and nights we shared
in tropical places
and how you'd only see me among
many pretty faces
The strength you possess when times are tough
The willingness to help others
when your days are rough
Your growing faith which is anchored to the core
Your patience as life gets back to the way before
Being an example to the world and your sons
so they can follow your path when
the Lord says "well done"

Lisa McGhee Smith

Honey, the love and commitment you
have to our family
and especially the love you have for me,
is why I thank God for you everyday
and particularly this
September 3rd—our 14th wedding anniversary!

Thoughts of a Daydreamer

How Much Do You Love Me?

If my car broke down and I needed a ride home
Would you come get me or send someone else?

What if I had a horrible day at work
Would you listen patiently as I spoke?

What if I over slept again
Would you have my clothes ready and
something to eat before I left?

What if you were "in the mood"
Would you let me keep sleeping soundly?

What if I came up short financially
Would you pay my bills without hesitation?

What if that comment you said hurt me so badly
Would you apologize and really mean it?

What if I were sick and couldn't
take care of myself
Would you be there and take care
of all my needs?

And what if this life is not long
enough to express our love
Would you look for me in the next?

How much do you love me?

Lisa McGhee Smith

Show Me How

Our paths cross everyday
You look at me then you look away

I know you see the hunger in my eyes
The permission I give with my smile

What do you see when you glance at me
I am one who just wants to complete thee

I want you to show me how
to make your heart skip a beat
when you detect my presence on the street

I want you to show me how
to imprison your eyes to lock their focus
on my lips, my breasts, my thighs

I want you to show me how,
with one soft kiss, make your body tingle
with thoughts of anticipated bliss

I want you to show me how
to take care of your every need
from loving you tenderly to providing a
patient ear and soft shoulder to vent a bad deed

I want you to show me how
to be your friend
Someone you can trust and count on
to the very end

When our paths cross again
say yes to my smile's invitation
to feed the hunger in my eyes

Tease me, take me, teach me
to be all the woman you need me to be

Thoughts of a Daydreamer

What Is It About You?

What is it about you that makes
me want to smile?
What is it about you that makes
me run for miles?

What is it about you that makes
my heart skip a beat?
What is it about you that makes
my body feel heat?

What is it about you that lets me
stare into your eyes?
What is it about you that makes
me ignore other guys?

What is it about you that makes
me feel so proud?
What is it about you when
I scream your name out loud?

What is it about you that gently
calls my name?
What is it about you that daily
love is the same?

What is it about you that feels
safe wrapped in your arms?
What is it about you when I can't
resist your charm?

Lisa McGhee Smith

What is it about you that makes
you sexy and confident?
What is it about you that confirms
you were God-sent?

What is it about you that others
try to imitate?
What is it about you that
defines soul mate?

Thoughts of a Daydreamer

General

Thoughts of a Daydreamer
Hello Brother
My Space
Tests
Pleasantville
Will You Step Away?
Pseudosuicide
Dreams
Journey Around the Sun

Lisa McGhee Smith

Thoughts of a Daydreamer

The voices begin to fade
and the vision becomes unfocused

I hear their words but
I know not what they are saying

I see arms moving and people walking
Where they are going, I am ignorant

Then the thoughts begin to invade

At times, I replay memorable
experiences from my youth
Sometimes, I am living a life based on different
choices I've made

There are times when I repeat earlier
conversations but say what I
really wanted to say
And there are times when I am
so far in the future
that I am conversing with my grandchildren

During these times of tuning out, zoning out,
vegging out…daydreaming
poetic expressions are conceived
I am impregnated with scores of new thoughts, expressions and observations

And when I labor back to the present
state of reality
I must give birth to poetry

Thoughts of a Daydreamer

Hello Brother

Brother,
I see you heading in my direction
I watch you walk regally with such
confidence that its intimidating

Whether you realize it or not, you are a
representative of our past, present and future

I see so many titles and roles
wrapped up in you...
father, friend, lover, husband,
provider, past king, future leader, role model,
counselor, advisor, protector

I see strength in you

When you walk by, I want to say hello
to let you know I acknowledge who you
are and what you represent

My greeting is my way of thanking
you for representing
me, my family, my people

I want to look in your eyes, through
the windows of your soul, to deposit my approval
and gratitude and withdraw some strength to carry
me yet another day

So Brother,
When I speak to you, please accept this
gesture for what it is...
acknowledgement of a king

Hello Brother

Lisa McGhee Smith

My Space

I feel crowded
everyone wants my space

You have your own space
why do you want mine too?

Keep walking, pass me by
don't sit next to me

There is not enough space
for you and me both

Why do you force yourself into my space?
because I smiled? Said hello?

Go away
This is my space

I only want to inhale the air in my space
not to breathe your air in its place

Please leave my space

I deserve my space
I've earned my space

I want my space
I NEED my space!

Thoughts of a Daydreamer

Tests

My knowledge of the subject matter
is measured with the alphabet

Successful quizzing is measured
by how fast I can rattle off correct answers
to my whereabouts

My understanding of the point being made is measured by
an affirmative answer to every question asked

My commitment to the relationship is measured by the
right actions in a given situation

How often will my word not be good enough?
Why do I have to then prove it?

How often will my feelings not speak enough?
Why do I have to then say it?

How often will my desire not be visible enough?
Why do I have to then show it?

Tests never uncover the true depth of knowledge,
understanding or commitment
They just reveal what was memorized
for the present time

Lisa McGhee Smith

Pleasantville

i think i'll stay right here
with pleasant thoughts, hope and optimism
i like it up here with joy, buoyancy and cheer
i like walking on air postureful with bounce

i do not want to come down there
with pessimism, discouragement and gloom
that place is lonely, sad and dreary
there i walk with heavy weight
bending my back

today i choose to stay in my present state
of happiness i do not wish to leave this place
if i decide to visit your place i cannot stay long
it blinds my sight, chokes my breath,
begins to take my life

i'm sorry my visits have not been as frequent
but I like it up here
i invite you to come visit me soon

Thoughts of a Daydreamer

Will You Step Away?

I see you standing alone waiting
What are you waiting on?
Who are you waiting for?

If I come to you and ask your name
Will you step away?
Am I invading your space?

If I reach to touch your hand,
your hair, your face
Will you step away?
Am I invading your space?

If I come closer to smell your sweet scent
and bask in your aura
Will you step away?
Am I invading your space?

If I ask to go where you are going
Will you step away?
Am I invading your space?

If I ask what turns you on
Will you step away?
Am I invading your space?

If I ask again who are you waiting for
Will you step closer and say…"you"

Lisa McGhee Smith

Pseudosuicide

going for a ride
be back in a little while
don't know where I'm going
just for a drive

close the door, strap on the belt and drive away
been riding for along time
picked up two hitchhikers-peace and quiet
they don't say much but I want them around

been riding for a long time
got to go back, need to go back,
don't want to go back

back there is dead to me
deceased, defunct, departed

gonna keep on this ride
committing this pseudosuicide
'til I can get back to my support
that's spread wide
and everything that distresses me has died

Thoughts of a Daydreamer

Dreams

in the years of my youth...
summer days were filled with laziness
and daydreams

life crawled by at a snail's pace with my feet
dangling in a cool stream

hours upon hours of playing house or hopscotch
with a piece of broken glass

day after day of creating memories that would
eventually make up my past

with every dream, the details might change
but the end would be filled
with excitement, travels and love
and the stories shared with an enormous
audience of family and friends

...my wealth would be vast shared by all in need
from the first to the last
...my best friend would be the love of my life
supporting me in whatever I'd do
...my children would be smart, cute and
numerous—give or take a few

Lisa McGhee Smith

but sometimes dreams are just dreams
life's way of giving you hope
to continue preparing and planning for a life
instead of giving up to elope

sometimes dreams are just dreams
as you are equipped for the hunt
but feeling like you are the only
dream participant

sometimes dreams are just dreams

Thoughts of a Daydreamer

Journey Around the Sun

You've returned from your journey
around the sun
365 days it took to get it done

Each day filled with a different view
A unique sight all brand new

You took knowledge from each day
discerning what information you'd take
and what would stay

All to prepare yourself for the next trek
of 365 days in length

A journey around the sun
with a bit more wisdom and a lot more strength

Happy Birthday

Lisa McGhee Smith

Give the gift of poetry!
"*Thoughts of a Daydreamer*"
By Lisa McGhee Smith

"Lisa McGhee Smith is...visionary."
—**Dr. Dorothy Height**, Congressional Gold Medal Recipient and author of ***Open Wide the Freedom Gates***

Order online today at Amazon.com or use the form below

—**Order Form**—
Please print

Name: _____
Address: _____
City/State/Zip Code: _____
Daytime telephone number: _____
Number of Books: _____ @ **$20.00**
    (Price includes shipping and handling within the U.S.)
Total Due: $ _____
   <u>*Please make checks or money orders payable to*</u>: **Lisa Smith**

<u>**Mail Order Form To:**</u>
Lisa McGhee Smith,
120 Wyngate Way,
Fayetteville, GA 30215

Thank you for reading
Thoughts of a Daydreamer

Readers are encouraged to contact author Lisa McGhee Smith with questions or comments via email at lisapt1988@aol.com

Now Available!

A Powerful Christian Book for the Entire Family

"SIMPLY AMAZING! Brother Steve Kendall is on fire for Christ! Each chapter is so gripping that you just cannot put it down."

—Dr. Lucius M. Dalton, Senior Pastor, Mt. Moriah Baptist Church and author of *Doing What God Requires*

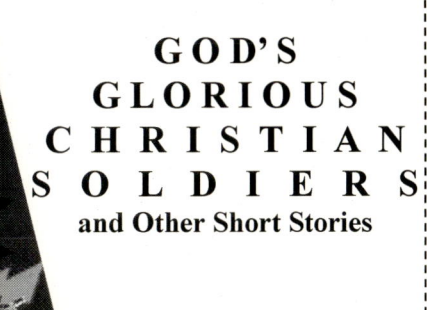

GOD'S GLORIOUS CHRISTIAN SOLDIERS
and Other Short Stories

The new book by Christian author Steven D. Kendall

Read excerpts and order online today!:
www.BibleStudyCafe.com